May your Mother's Day make you
smile and your heart blossom.

When a child is born so is a Grandmother!

When a child is born so is a Grandmother!

Grandmothers hold our tiny hands
for just a while, but our hearts forever.

Grandmothers hold our tiny hands
for just a while, but our hearts forever.

A Grandmother always has love
to give and time to spare.
A Grandmother is always there.

We love you to the moon and back!

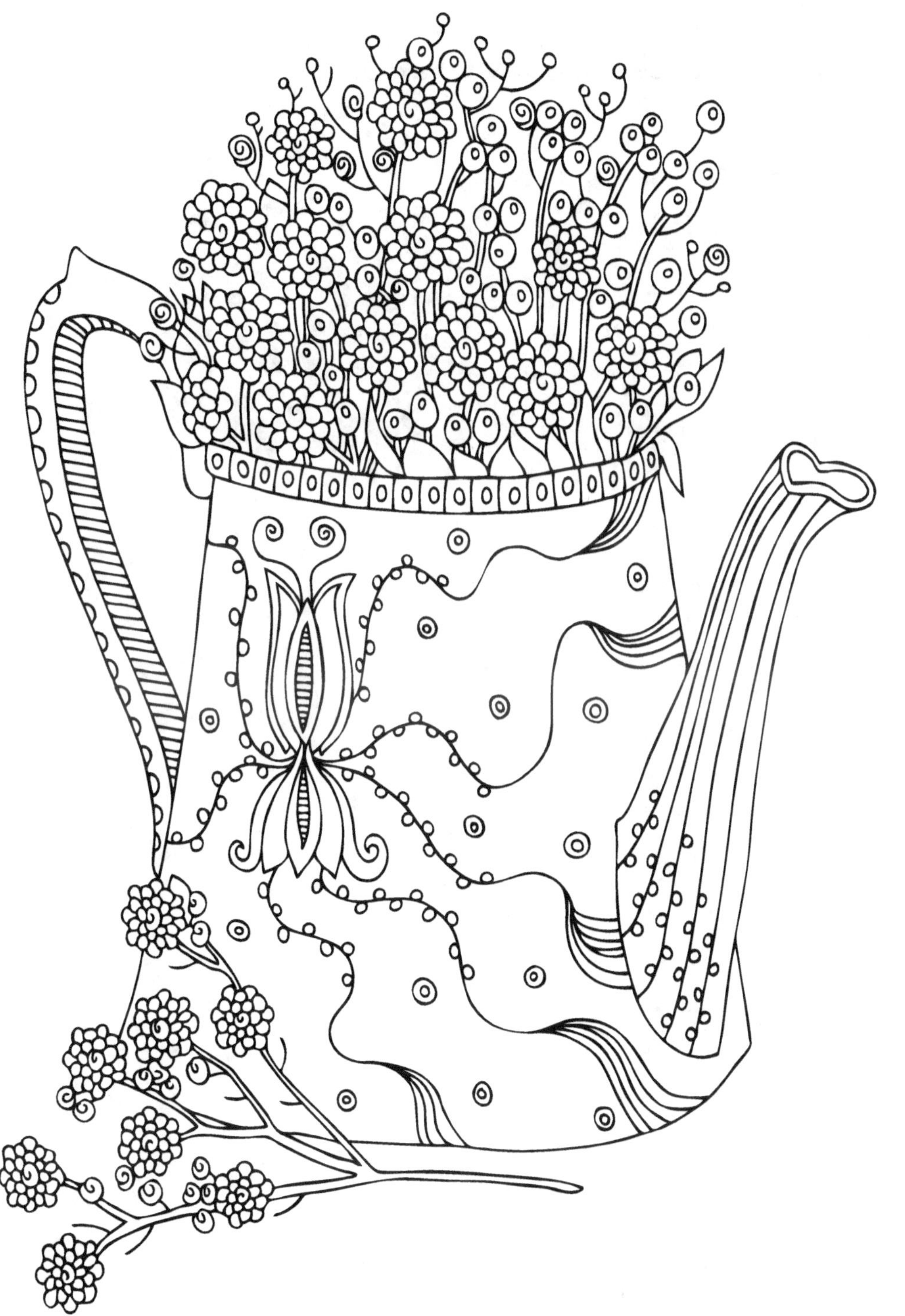

May your Mother's Day be as
bright and beautiful as you are!

You are always in my heart.

I love you from the top of my head
To the tips of my toes!

I love you from the top of my head
To the tips of my toes!

Every day is special with a
Grandmother like you.

Grandmothers are moms with lots of frosting!

Grandmothers are moms with lots of frosting!

A Grandma's love feels like nobody else's.

A Grandma's love feels like nobody else's.

May all of your dreams come true.

May all of your dreams come true.

flowers for your special day!

flowers for your special day!

Wishing you a day that is
just like you want it to be!

Happy Mother's Day to the

Best Grandmother!

(Coloring Card)

Copyright 2018

from

____